Ready-to-Go Comprehension

Easy Activities for All Readers

by Terri Heidger & Beth Stevens, The Apron Ladies

Ready-to-Go Comprehension: Easy Activities for All Readers
By Terri Heidger and Beth Stevens

Cover and Interior Design: Charmaine Whitman
Design Elements: Shutterstock

Library of Congress Cataloging-in-Publication Data
Cataloging-in-Publication information is on file with the Library of Congress.
978-1-4966-0532-0 (pbk.)
978-1-4966-0533-7 (eBook PDF)

Capstone Professional publishes professional resources for K–12 educators.
Contact us for tailored, in-school training or to schedule an author for a workshop or conference.
Visit www.capstonepd.com for free lesson plan downloads.

Maupin House Publishing, Inc. by Capstone Professional
1710 Roe Crest Drive
North Mankato, MN 56003
www.capstonepd.com
888-262-6135
proposals@capstonepd.com

Table of Contents

Introduction

We were excited to bring you *Ready-to-Go Comprehension: Easy Activities for All Readers*. In *Become a Good Reader: Six Simple Steps*, we compare learning to read to "doing a dance." In this new and revised handbook, we continue that dance as we share strategies and activities that will help your students gain meaning from the text they are reading.

We are teachers, too, and all of the strategies and activities that we are sharing with you are ones that we have used in our very own classrooms. This handbook was written to support and encourage you as teachers in the process of teaching comprehension to your students.

As teachers, we understand that time is a precious commodity, which makes it important to find the right resources on instructional methods. So we wrote this handbook as a very instructive and easy-to-use resource for teaching different types of comprehension strategies. We describe the comprehension strategies that successful readers use consistently before, during, and after reading to gain meaning from text. The nine comprehension strategies and a brief description of each are below.

③ Visualizing: Students use sensory descriptions in a text to create visual images from it.

④ Questioning: Students question before, during, and after reading to monitor their comprehension of a text.

⑤ Clarifying/Monitoring: Students question whether something makes sense and use fix-up strategies to monitor their understanding.

⑥ Making Connections: Students connect what they are reading to themselves, other texts they've read, or what they know about the world.

⑦ Inferring: Students go beyond the literal words on the page to better understand the text. They use evidence from the text and their own prior knowledge to do so.

⑧ Summarizing: Students recall the important details of a text in their own words.

Activities

It is important for us as teachers to reinforce these strategies repeatedly and to provide multiple opportunities for students to learn, practice, and assimilate them. We provide you with three activities per strategy, for a total of 27 hands-on and interactive reading comprehension activities. We have used all of them with success in our classrooms to create readers who understand what they read.

We hope that you find our activities to be motivating and fun as you adapt them to suit your own classroom. That's what good teachers do each and every day!

The 9 Strategies

1 **Using Prior Knowledge:** Students think about what they already know about a topic of a text to make deeper connections to the text.

2 **Predicting:** Students use their background knowledge and what they acquired from the text to predict what they will read or what will happen next in the text.

9 **Evaluating:** Students make judgments about the text and learn that stronger texts have more evidence.

Using This Book

Throughout this book, the word **SAY** identifies those questions that model an appropriate strategy. These questions are metacognitive in that they teach our students to "think about what they are thinking about." You should ask your students these questions as a way to provide feedback that helps them to comprehend what they are reading and encourages them not only to think about what they are reading, but also to have conversations with their peers and with you. These research-based strategies have been adapted from several respected sources, including Regie Routman, Tanny McGregor, Debbie Miller, Janet Allen, Gretchen Owocki, Irene C. Fountas, and Gay Su Pinnell. They were then refined and used by both of us in our classrooms. Each strategy is introduced and presented with a variety of enjoyable activities that reinforce it.

1 Using Prior Knowledge

Access students' prior knowledge of a topic by having them think about, relate to, and recall facts about the topic. The goal is to have students tap into their schema and cue in on information that they are reminded of as they begin to discuss the text.

Activities

ABC LIST COUNTDOWN

Students list the letters of the alphabet on a sheet of paper and write a word for each letter that relates to the topic they are reading beginning with each letter. For example, for the topic Dinosaurs, they might write *Brontosaurus* for the letter *B* and *Carnivore* for the letter *C* (see Illustrations on p. 24). Students brainstorm for about five minutes. They

SAY:

"Look at boldface headings and subheadings if it is a nonfiction text. You must also look at pictures, diagrams, or charts. What do these remind you of? Tap into your background knowledge."

"Look at the title of the text and the front and back cover. You can read the first and last paragraph of the text. Does it remind you of another text you have read in the past?"

"We are now going to brainstorm everything that comes to mind before reading this book about… (e.g., fairies, sharks)."

share their responses with the class as you write their words on the board, displaying them on the document camera or whiteboard. Allow students to discuss what they know about the topic with their table partners.

TRUE OR FALSE?

Create one TRUE and one FALSE card for each student in your class, and prepare true and false statements to activate your students' prior knowledge of the topic they will be reading. The statements need to be general enough so that students can answer them even before reading the text. For example, for the topic of Dinosaurs, you could say "Dinosaurs died a long time ago" and "Dinosaurs all ate plants." After reading each statement, have each student hold up a TRUE or FALSE card as a response. This will provide you with immediate feedback about your students' knowledge of the topic and allow you to monitor their progress.

KNOW IT! THINK I KNOW IT! NO CLUE!

Prepare a three-column chart with the headings *Know It, Think I Know It,* and *No Clue* for each student in your class. Then write on the board 20 keywords related to the text the students will be reading about. Have the students write each word under the heading that represents their own personal knowledge of the word. Use this individualized activity to let students know what they don't know. After completing the reading of the text, ask students to revisit their three-column chart and revise their responses in another color pen or pencil.

2 Predicting

Predicting teaches students to gaze into their crystal balls in order to bring meaning to information that has not yet been read. To do this, students activate their prior knowledge. Making predictions is an ongoing strategy that students are taught to utilize before and during reading. When predicting, students are constantly employing their background knowledge and combining it with information they acquire from the text.

Activities

CRYSTAL CONFIRMATIONS

Have students create their own "crystal ball" by decorating a small, square tissue box. Then after activating your students' prior knowledge using the **SAY** questions, pass out small strips of paper to each student. The students write three or four predictions beginning with the phrase "I predict that..." then place the predictions into their "crystal

SAY:

"What might you learn?"

"What inferences can you make from the pictures, illustrations, and cover?"

"What do you think the book is going to be about?"

"Do you think this book will be fiction or nonfiction?"

balls." As they read the text, have students come back to their crystal balls to confirm or reject their predictions. Encourage students to continue making predictions as they read and to keep a tally of how many of their predictions came true.

ARTISTIC ASSUMPTIONS

Take a "picture walk" with your students, and activate their prior knowledge by discussing the title, author, genre, and content of the text they will be reading. Give each student in your class one index card that has been folded in half so that there is a vertical crease running down the middle of the card (see Illustrations on p. 24). On one side of the index card, have your students write a prediction beginning with the phrase "I predict…" and on the other side, have them explain their prediction beginning with the word "Because…" After reading the text, students should return to their predictions to see if they were correct.

WHAT'S MY BEST GUESS?

We need to continually teach our students to make predictions before they read and as they read based on text evidence and picture clues. Create a simple template for your students to be used with any text.

Based on the cover, I predict…

As I read the text I discover that…

After reading the text, I learned that…

Circle your reflection.

My prediction was correct.

My prediction was incorrect.

Take a few minutes to share the students' "best guesses" with the entire class.

3 Visualizing

This strategy teaches students to use all of their senses while reading. Creating visual and other sensory images from text during and after reading is a comprehension strategy that successful readers of all ages use routinely when they read to construct meaning. Hint: Bring in realia to allow students to taste, feel, see, touch, and smell different objects. Students will enjoy experiencing these sensory images firsthand, and together you and your students will have a classroom rich in imagination and descriptive vocabulary.

Activities

NAME THAT SENSE

Prepare index cards with characters or events from the text and their matching descriptions. Have students pair up, and give each pair a description card. Students discuss what they visualize when they read the cards and what was going on in the text at that time.

SAY:

"What do you see in your mind?"

"What can you hear?"

"What can you feel?"

"What can you taste or smell?"

Variation: Have students incorporate the descriptions into their writing as a way to spice it up with sensory images.

WHAT'S IN MY SUITCASE?

Students are to close their eyes and visualize what they may pack in their suitcases if they were to visit a place described in one of their texts. Be sure to choose a text rich in description and read a page or two. Then give your students the opportunity to write or sketch what they might pack. For example, read a descriptive paragraph from *Polar Regions* by Melanie Waldron, published by Capstone (2013). (There are many fiction and nonfiction texts written about different types of regions.) DON'T give them the title of the book. Have them use their senses to visualize and jot down their ideas. Once again, it is important to give your students time to share their responses. Modeling, practicing, and sharing are vital for teaching our students to becoming critical thinkers!

PAINT A PICTURE

Have your students close their eyes as you read a very descriptive passage or poem filled with rich, colorful language. Then have students draw a picture of the mental image they formed while listening to the text. Students may volunteer to share their illustrations with a partner, a small group, or the whole class. Continue to use this activity periodically throughout the reading of the text to get students to form mental images of the story.
Variation: Play a drawing and guessing game with students. After students have read a text, one student chooses a passage that he or she will silently draw. The rest of the class tries to guess the part of the passage based on the illustration.

④ Questioning

Asking questions helps students to organize their thoughts, utilize and build their prior knowledge, and confirm or reject the predictions they have previously made. In addition, questioning also helps students clarify what they are reading, move more deeply into the text, and decide what is important as they read.

Activities

QUESTIONING CUBES

You will need several one-inch plastic cubes and sticker dots that fit them. Label your stickers with the question stems *Who?*, *What?*, *Where?*, *When?*, *Why?*, and *How?*, and place them on one plastic cube. Label six more stickers with the helping verbs *can*, *did*, *is*, *will*, *would*, and *might*, and attach these dots to another plastic cube. Pair up your students and provide each pair with one question stem and one helping verb cube. (See Illustrations on p. 24.)

SAY:

"Can you agree or disagree with your prediction?"

"What questions do you have as you read the text?"

"Try using these question stems as you ask:
'I wonder…'
'What if…'"

"Where can you find the answers?"

"As you are reading, remember to ask yourself these key questions: Who? What? Where? When? Why? How?"

Read aloud from the text your students are reading, then have your students take turns rolling the cubes and asking each other questions about the text using the two rolled words. Be sure to model this activity so that students understand the concept of formulating meaningful questions.

FILE FOLDER FACTS

Depending on your class and your teaching style, you can either create a large cut-out of an object, character, or setting that represents the story you are reading (e.g., a picture of the dog from *Because of Winn-Dixie* by Kate DiCamillo, published by Candlewick) OR give each student a manila folder. Assign parts of the story for students to read, and give them questions about this section of the story to write on sticky notes (e.g., How does Opal feel about finding Winn Dixie in the grocery store?). Once the students have read the assigned pages, have them answer the questions on their sticky notes and post them on the cut-out of the story or write them directly into their file folder. Once again,

it is very important that you model, practice, and share the strategy of questioning through think alouds using the question stems. Then encourage students to come up with their own questions and add them to their manila folders. Have students answer their own questions. Students can use their responses to summarize the text, create a book report, or prepare to take an assessment.

COMPREHENSION QUICK-CHECK

Pass out four or five sticky notes to each student. As they read, have students write questions about the text on these sticky notes. After students have read independently for a specified amount of time (you can determine the time based on the text), ask a student to read to the class one of the questions written on his or her sticky notes. Then choose another student to answer this question. Continue randomly selecting students to ask and answer questions. This activity allows all students to be actively engaged in their reading and allows you to monitor their comprehension quickly and easily.

5 Clarifying/Monitoring

Students must monitor for understanding in order for meaningful comprehension to take place. If they are unsure about a concept or a specific vocabulary word, the entire piece of text becomes unclear and metacognition cannot occur. Not only must we give our readers the strategies they need in order to make meaning, but we need to give them the permission to say, "This doesn't make sense." It is our job as teachers to help them bridge that gap between learning to read and reading to learn. Clarifying and monitoring are great tools to help our students make those connections.

Activities

TALK ABOUT IT

Draw a thought bubble/speech bubble on a piece of construction paper. Laminate it. Cut out the center of the bubble and laminate the speech

SAY:

"What part was tricky for you?"

"Does that make sense?"

"What is a question that you have about the text?"

"What are you wondering about as you read?"

"Can you show me the part that confused you?"

"Does it make sense now?"

bubble again, which creates a window effect. Our students love using their thought bubbles in kindergarten through grade 5. As you are reading your text in small group, stop and ask the students what they are thinking, or ask what things they have questions about. Be sure to include all of the question stems in our **SAY** section as well as any that you'd like to include. They love taking turns holding up the thought bubble and sharing their thoughts and questions. This is a great activity to practice clarifying and monitoring as students can work together to clarify their understanding or they can be prompted to read on to find the answer to a question they may have.

AHA! HUH?

As students read, have them stop and jot down two Ahas! and one Huh? (something they still have a question about or something that needs further clarification). Take time at the end of your small reading group to share and discuss all of your students Ahas! and Huhs? Since students will be providing their feedback in the form of text evidence, it will be helpful to see whether there are any misunderstandings about the text. This is a very quick but powerful activity that, again, lets students know that it is OK to be unclear. And it is an important way for you to know what your students are still struggling with.

DEAR STUDENT

Have students write a six-sentence note to another student. Their notes must include two key points that they learned from the text and one key point that is still confusing to them. They will enjoy writing their notes, and their peers will enjoy reading them. You can also check the letters to monitor their learning and their questions!

6 Making Connections

Making a connection to the text is a strategy that students can use before, during, and after reading. Personal connections enhance students' learning and help them relate to events and characters in the stories and expository text that they read.

Activities

THE *AHA!* TREE

This is a great interactive addition to your classroom and can be adapted to every text at each grade level. Create a large tree on a bulletin board in your classroom. As students make connections to the text (text-to-text, text-to-self, and text-to-world), have them write down and illustrate their connections to hang on the tree. Be sure to model this activity using a well-known story. For example, in *Because of Winn-Dixie*, Opal becomes very upset when she can't find her dog. A connection might include a drawing of a person crying and the phrases, "I lost my dog once,

SAY:

"What does this remind you of?"

"Are you making a text-to-text connection?"

"Are you making a text-to-self connection?"

"Are you making a text-to-world connection?"

"When I read the part about...it reminded me of..."

"When I saw the picture, I thought of..."

"Have I read or seen this before in another book?"

and I was afraid that I would never see him again. I was really upset." Scaffold students who write general things like "I have a dog" by encouraging them to connect that experience with the book. Place a bell by the tree and have each student ring it and shout "Aha!" when he or she puts a connection on the tree. (The bell is optional for those who prefer a quieter environment.)

MAKING MEMORIES

Have each student bring in a small box, and divide it into three sections labeled TEXT-TO-TEXT, TEXT-TO-SELF, and TEXT-TO-WORLD. This will serve as a "memory box." Whenever students are reading, either independently or in a small or large group, ask them to make at least one connection to the text. Have the students write down this connection on a piece of paper and place it in the corresponding section of their memory box. At the end of the year, this memory box will remind students of the connections they have made to the different texts they read throughout the year.

CONNECTION COLLECTION

Create a simple template that you can use for multiple texts. Include these three sentence stems.

Text-to-Text: *How do the ideas in this text remind you of another text, movie, or song? Complete one of the following stems.*

- What I just read reminds me of _____ because...
- The ideas in this text are similar to the ideas in _____ because...

Text-to-Self: *How do the ideas in this text relate to your own experiences? Complete one of the following stems.*

- This reminds me of a time I...
- I understand or agree with the author because in my life...

Text-to-World: *How do the ideas in this text relate to an event that has or is taking place in the world? Complete one of the following stems.*

- What I just read reminds me of _____ that I read in the newspaper or saw on the news today.
- What I just read makes me think about _____ that happened in the past because...

Also post the sentences above in a Making Connections poster for students to refer to.

7 Inferring

Inferring means making a best guess about a part of the text that goes beyond the literal words on the page. Good readers are constantly inferring as they read by predicting, using their schema, and using clues from the text. These include facts and opinions, text evidence, and text structures, such as cause and effect. Reading between the lines gives those literal thinkers the opportunity to make decisions and judgments about the text they are reading in a short amount of time. We need to remember that this strategy takes time to learn and needs to be practiced daily. Remember to make your lessons memorable and fun filled!

SAY:

"What can you infer about...?"

"What was the text evidence that helped you make this inference?"

"What do you already know?"

"I predict... I infer..."

"Could this mean...?"

Activities

WILD CARD

Collect an assortment of pictures from online or from magazines. These pictures can be an assortment of animals, superheroes, sports, holidays, or any theme under study. Have a pile of cards and a container of chips. Call a student to the front of the room, and give him or her a picture card and 3 chips.

IMPORTANT: He or she may not look at the card.
The student then holds up the picture card for the rest of the class to see. Students will take turns giving the cardholder clues about the picture. The cardholder will use his or her schema to make a guess about the picture. After each guess, the student puts a chip back in the container. He or she has three chances to make a guess.

This activity provides students with a fun opportunity to use their deductive-reasoning and critical-thinking skills. What a simple way to teach inferring! Just as students used what they know and the clues from their classmates to make an inference, they'll use what they know and clues from the text to make inferences as they read. You can provide a simple graphic organizer with the following heads to fill out as they read: *What You Know, Clues from the Text, Inference.*

WHAT HAT AM I WEARING?

Show students pictures of different types of hats. Some examples include a sports cap, a lady's fancy hat, a type of helmet, and a fedora. As you read a text about a fictional character or person from real life, have students discuss what type of hat that person would wear and select evidence from the text that explains why he or she would wear that hat. Encourage students to make an inference using that person's behavior in the text.

READ BETWEEN THE LINES

Choose your favorite read-aloud or picture book. Make a set of index cards with the words *Agree* and *Disagree*. Give each student a set of cards. Begin by reading the first few lines of the text, and then STOP and ask students to make a good guess using the inferring stems under **SAY**. Quickly note their responses on chart paper or whiteboard. Continue reading a few more paragraphs, then STOP and have students Agree or Disagree with their previous inferences. They must orally provide text evidence. Record their responses, and determine whether or not each is supported by the text. Readers need to practice the skill of inferring when the answers to their questions are not directly stated in the text.

8 Summarizing

Students synthesize the text and restate it in their own words, either orally or in writing, to reinforce and assimilate what they have read and learned. The ability to summarize text is vital to good student comprehension.

Activities

SOMEBODY...WANTED...BUT...SO

This activity has been adapted for classroom use from Project CRISS. Model the activity for your students before asking them to complete it independently. Prepare an activity sheet with the headings SOMEBODY, WANTED, BUT, and SO. Modeling the story *Cinderella*, under SOMEBODY, write *Cinderella*; under WANTED, write *to go to the ball*; under BUT, write *her stepmother would not let her go to the ball*; and under SO, write *her fairy godmother came along and cast a magic spell so Cinderella could go to the ball, and Cinderella and the prince lived happily ever*

SAY:

"Did you understand what you read?"

"If you cannot summarize or retell what you have read, go back and reread the parts that are tricky for you."

"Can you retell in your own words...?"

"Can you explain...or can you give me more information about...?"

"Tell me what you have read in your own words. Does it make sense? Try to keep it short and sweet."

after. Now have your students complete the activity by summarizing the story they have read.

Variation: Students use the keywords on the activity sheet as a framework to orally retell the story to an assigned partner.

SHOEBOX SUMMARIES

This is a fun, creative way to summarize either a longer expository or narrative text. First, have students write a summary of the text they have read. Encourage students to write events of the story first and use that to create their summaries. Model as appropriate. Ask each student to bring in a shoebox with a lid, and provide the students with arts and crafts items, such as colored paper, crayons, markers, glue sticks, and glitter. Next, have the students use their supplies to recreate a specific part of the text. For example, students might make a favorite character, setting, or event from the story. Encourage students to be creative by adding their personal interpretation to their creation. Once students are done, have them place their creations in their shoebox, and display the shoeboxes around the classroom. Students can also practice their oral storytelling skills using their shoebox creations.

PICK A CARD…ANY CARD

This activity will help students summarize and generate questions for either narrative or expository text. Using index cards, label each card with one of the following phrases: *Who?, What?, Where?, When?, Why?, How?, Define and List, Explain, Compare, What If?, Summarize, Arrange,* and *What Caused?* Divide the class into groups of three to four students, and provide each group with one set of question word cards. Assign one student to be the "dealer," and have this student hold the cards spread out, fan-like, with the words facing inward. One student picks a card from the dealer and poses a question using the prompt word on the card about the text the class just read. Another group member answers the question. Continue this activity until each student has had at least two turns.

Variation: Students write their questions on paper and exchange them with another group.

9 Evaluating

It is important to teach our readers to constantly monitor their comprehension by evaluating what they have read. When they evaluate a text, they make judgments about the text, the ideas, the author's point of view, and other elements of the author's craft. Readers will soon discover that stronger texts have lots of evidence to back up claims. It is helpful when evaluating texts to have students write a written response, as they will be looking for and using evidence from the text to back up their claims.

Activities

EXIT SLIPS

A great activity that will allow you and your students to evaluate their learning is with Exit Slips. Decide what you'd like to find out about the students' learning at the end of the lesson. Write a question or pose a problem on the board, and have them respond on an Exit Slip. Consider using the questions under **SAY** and select one to write on

SAY:

"Tell me what's important about what you read without telling too much."

"What part did you like the best? Why?"

"What questions do you still have?"

"What part or parts were confusing?"

"What is the author saying?"

"Does the author say it clearly? Why or Why not?"

"Could the author have said it better? How?"

the board for students to respond to on a sheet of paper. At the end of the day, have students respond to the question. Then stand at the door, and collect the Exit Slips or have the students post their slips as they leave the classroom. Look at the students' Exit Slips carefully, and divide them into piles: Students who understand the concept, those who do not get the concept, and those who you may not be sure about. Begin your next day's lesson reviewing the responses on selected Exit Slips.

20-WORD SUMMARY

This is a great activity for students to use to evaluate and synthesize what they have read in a short period of time. The power is in the process of being able to say it in a summary of 20 words or less while also critiquing the book. Students love sharing their writing with a table partner. They can then critique, discuss, or evaluate each other's thoughts. Again, this is an activity that will need to be modeled, practiced, and shared so that students learn what is important and what is not important in a critique.

WHERE'S MY EVIDENCE?

Students love to Stop and Jot as they read and after they have completed reading a piece of text. Provide students with sticky notes. Pose a question about the text you are reading either as a group or independently. Students are then asked to Stop and Jot their evaluations, making judgments supported by strong text evidence. They are to use one of the following terms when jotting each response:

Because…

For instance…

For example…

The author said…

According to the text,

From the reading,
I know that…

It said on page _____
that…

Illustrations

ABC List Countdown
STRATEGY #1

DINOSAURS

- **A**mazing
- **B**rontosaurus, big
- **C**arnivore
- **D**eadly
- **E**xtinct
- **F**erocious
- **G**
- **H**
- **I**
- **J**
- **K**
- **L**arge
- **M**ajestic

- **N**
- **O**
- **P**owerful
- **Q**
- **R**aptor
- **S**
- **T**yrannosaurus rex
- **U**
- **V**icious
- **W**ondrous
- **X**
- **Y**
- **Z**

Artistic Assumptions
STRATEGY #2

Tyler	
I predict that it is Anne's birthday	because I see pictures for going places.

Questioning Cubes
STRATEGY #4